BALTO

The Dog Who Saved Nome

By Margaret Davidson

Illustrated by Cathie Bleck

SCHOLASTIC INC.

New York   Toronto   London   Auckland   Sydney

The story "Balto, The Dog who Saved Nome" is from *Five True Dog Stories*, originally published by Scholastic Inc.
This reillustrated version was originally published in SCHOLASTIC LITERACY PLACE®.

Text copyright © 1977 by Margaret Davidson.
Illustrations copyright © 1996 by Scholastic Inc.
All rights reserved. Published by Scholastic Inc.

Printed in the U.S.A.
ISBN 0-590-22907-9

    6 7 8 9 10 11   40   09 08 07

"THIS IS NOME, ALASKA. REPEAT. THIS IS NOME, ALASKA. WE NEED HELP. FAST..."

A man bent over the machine in the Nome telegraph office. Again and again he pressed down the signal key. *Click-click-clack ... Clack-click-clack ...* He was sending a message to the town of Anchorage, Alaska, 800 miles to the south.

Click-click-clack ... Clack-click-clack ... The Anchorage telegraph operator wrote down the message. The news was very bad.

A terrible sickness had broken out in the Nome area—a disease called diphtheria. Some people had already died of it. Many more would die if they weren't treated soon.

There was no medicine to treat diphtheria in Nome. The medicine they needed would have to come from Anchorage—800 miles away—through a wild wind and snow storm. The storm was so bad that airplanes couldn't fly through it. Trains couldn't get through either. Nome was very near the sea, but the sea was frozen solid. And the road from the south was completely blocked by deep drifts of snow.

There was only one way to get the medicine from Anchorage to Nome—by dogsled.

The medicine was packed in a box and sent north by train—as far as a train could go on the snowy tracks. It was still more than 600 miles south of Nome. From now on teams of dogs would have to take it the rest of the way.

The teams were ready. The first team pushed north through the storm to a little town. There a second team was waiting. It went on to another small town where a third team was ready to take the medicine on north.

At first the teams managed to go many miles before they grew tired. But the storm was growing worse by the minute. Finally Charlie Olson's team staggered into the little village of Bluff—60 miles south of Nome. They had only gone 20 miles, yet Olson and the dogs were almost frozen and completely worn out.

Gunnar Kasson and his team were waiting in Bluff. The wind screamed through the little town. The snow was piling up deeper and deeper on the ground. It was 30 degrees *below* zero Fahrenheit outside now. And the temperature was falling fast.

"It's no use trying to go out in *that*," Charlie Olson said. "I almost didn't make it. You and the dogs will freeze solid before you get half way."

But Kasson knew how important the medicine was. He knew that hundreds—maybe thousands—of people would die if they didn't get the medicine soon. Besides, he knew he didn't have to go all the way. Another team was waiting 40 miles north in the little village of Safety. That team would take the medicine the last 20 miles to Nome.

Quickly Gunnar Kasson hitched up his team of dogs. And at the head of the long line he put his lead dog, Balto.

Balto was a mixed-breed. He was half Eskimo dog—and half wolf. Many dogs who are part wolf never become tame. They never learn to trust people—or obey them either. Balto was different. He was a gentle dog who obeyed orders quickly. He also knew how to think for himself.

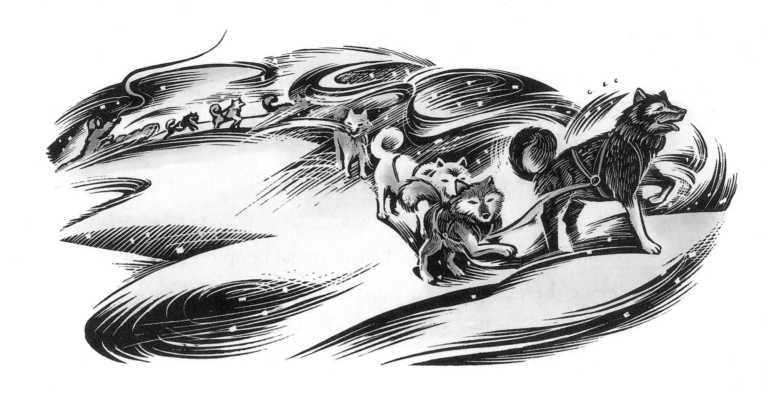

Usually Gunnar Kasson guided the dogs. He told them where to go. Now he couldn't even see his hand in front of his face. So everything was up to Balto. The big black dog would have to find the trail by smell. Then he'd have to stay on it no matter what happened.

Gunnar Kasson climbed onto the back of the sled. He cracked his whip in the air. "*Mush!*" he cried. "*Move out!*"

The first part of the trail to Nome led across the sea ice. This ice wasn't anything like ice on a small pond or lake. It seemed much more *alive*. And no wonder. The water *under* the ice was moving up and down because of the storm. So the ice was moving up and down too. Up and down, up and down it went, like a roller coaster.

In some places the ice was smooth—as smooth and slippery as glass. Dogs are usually sure-footed. But they slipped and skidded across this ice. So did the sled.

And sometimes the ice came to sharp points—points that dug deep into the dogs' paws.

Worst of all were the places where the ice was bumpy—so bumpy that the sled turned over again and again. Each time it turned over the other dogs began to bark and snap at each other. But Balto always stood quietly while Kasson set the sled upright again. Balto was calm, so the other dogs grew calmer too.

The team had been moving across the ice for hours.

Suddenly there was a loud *cracking* sound—like a gun going off. Kasson knew that sound. It was the sound of ice breaking. Somewhere not far ahead the ice had split apart. If the team kept going straight they would run right into the freezing water—and drown.

Balto heard the ice crack too. He slowed for a moment. Then he turned left. He headed straight out to sea. He went for a long time. Then he turned right once more.

Balto was leading the team *around* the icy water. Finally he gave a sharp bark and turned north. He had found the trail to Nome again.

Soon the trail left the sea ice. From now on it was over land. Things should have been easier. They weren't. The snow was falling thick and fast. In some places the wind swept most of it off the trail. But in other places the snow drifts came up almost over the dogs' heads. And the wind was blowing harder and harder. It sent bits of icy snow straight into Kasson's eyes. "I might as well have been blind," he said. "I couldn't even *guess* where we were."

And the dogs were so tired! Again and again they tried to stop. They wanted to lie down and go to sleep in the snow. Balto was just as tired. But he would not stop. He kept on pulling—and the other dogs had to follow behind.

Now something else began to worry Gunnar Kasson. They had been traveling for about 14 hours. Surely they should have reached the town of Safety in 14 hours. Kasson went on for another hour. Then he knew. Somehow they had missed the town in the storm. They must have passed right by the new dog team!

Kasson knew they couldn't stop and wait for the storm to die down. He and the dogs would freeze if they did. They couldn't go back to Bluff either. They had come too far. There was only one thing to do now. Pray ... and push on to Nome.

Later Gunnar Kasson said he couldn't remember those last miles very well. Each one was a nightmare of howling wind and swirling snow and bitter cold. But somehow—with Balto leading slowly and steadily—they made it! At 5:30 in the morning, February 2, 1925—after 20 hours on the trail—the team limped into Nome!

The whole town was waiting for the medicine! They gathered around Gunnar Kasson. They shook his hand and pounded him on the back. "How can we ever thank you?" one woman cried.

Gunnar Kasson shook his head. Then he sank to his knees beside Balto. He began to pull long splinters of ice from the dog's paws. "Balto, what a dog," he said. "I've been in Alaska for 20 years and this was the toughest trip I've ever made. But Balto, *he* brought us through."

Many newspaper and magazine stories were written about Balto. His picture was printed on postcards and in books. And today, on a grassy hill in New York City's Central Park, there is a life-sized statue of Balto—the dog who saved Nome.